BAD BIG SISTER

By Kiara Davies
Illustrated by Margarita Yeromina

Library For All Ltd.

2

My big sister is mean. She is a bad big sister.

She left me here. I wish that place never picked her!

3

She went to the big city to have fun and go to school.

But I think she went just to be cruel.

She told me, "Dakota, look after Ebony and Dean. Also, make sure my room stays clean."

Sometimes, I go in to her room and try on her clothes. I know she'd be mad, but she's not here, so she won't know.

18:32

'New message from: Kiara!'

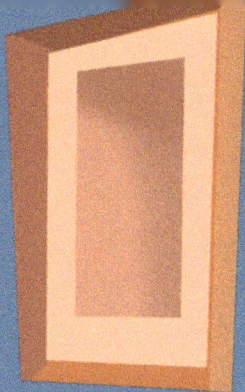

Ebony and Dean ask me to play, but I always tell them, "Go away!"

Kiara is a bad big sister, because I only see her 10 weeks every year. She makes me mad because she's never here.

She talks on Facetime to Mum and Dad, but I refuse because she is mean.

Mum says, "Boarding school is hard, but she is doing it for you." This makes me want to yell because I never asked her to!

Ebony and Dean ask me again to play.
But I yell at them again: "GO AWAY!"

Ebony looks at me, then looks at Dean. That's when she screams, "You're the bad big sister! You're the one who's mean!"

I burst into tears and run to Kiara's room. I slam the door shut with a thunderous *BOOM!*

Tap, tap, tap.

I dial her phone. When she picks up
I yell: "You left me alone!"

She stares back at me through the screen for a second, and the anger in me starts to lessen.

She says, "I'm sorry I left you, but there are no schools near our place. I was really lucky to get picked for this one."

She wipes her tears. I do too.

"I know it's hard for you," she says,
"to be the big sister."

That's when I realise: I'm not mad,
I just miss her.

So now when she calls, I make sure I listen, because it can't be easy in her position. She tells me the fun things she is learning at her new school.

And when Ebony and Dean ask me to play, I do what Kiara would do. "Okay, let's find a game!" I say.

I still miss her and sometimes I cry, but she is a good big sister.

And so am I.

You can use these questions to talk about this book with your family, friends and teachers.

What did you learn from this book?

Describe this book in one word. Funny? Scary? Colourful? Interesting?

How did this book make you feel when you finished reading it?

What was your favourite part of this book?

About the author

Kiara Davies is a Kamilaroi woman who grew up in Mungindi and currently lives in Melbourne. She loves talking with and helping her family. Kiara's favourite story as a child was *The Little Match Girl*.

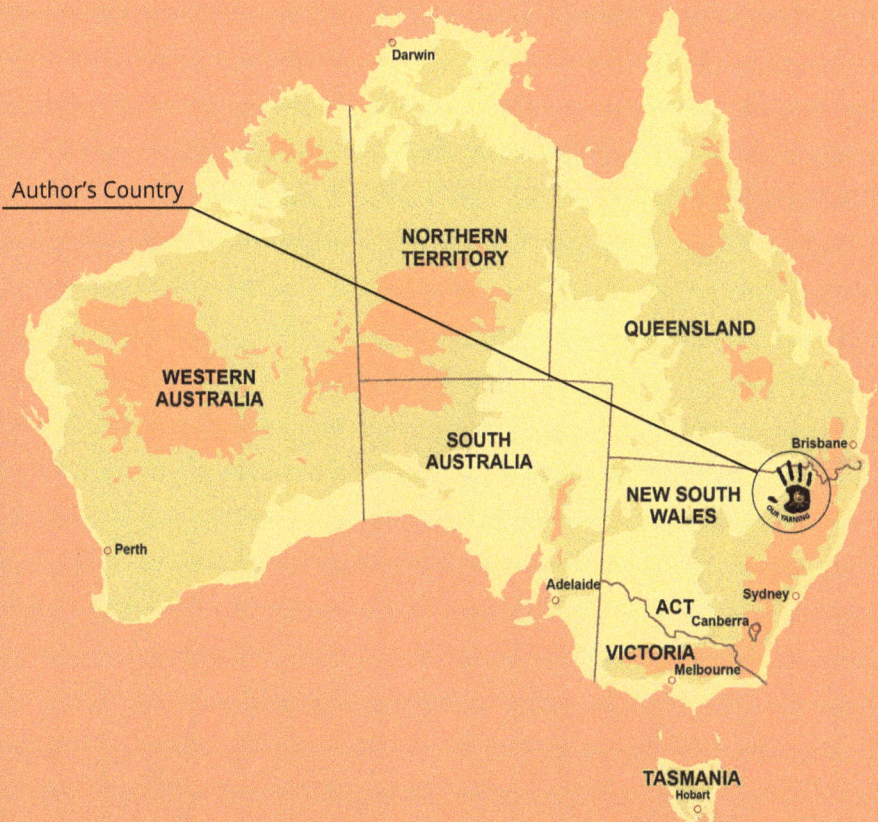

Author's Country

DARWIN

NORTHERN TERRITORY

QUEENSLAND

WESTERN AUSTRALIA

SOUTH AUSTRALIA

NEW SOUTH WALES

Brisbane

Perth

Adelaide

Sydney

ACT
Canberra

VICTORIA
Melbourne

TASMANIA
Hobart

Our Yarning

The Our Yarning collection aligns with the Australian Curriculum through the Cross-Curriculum Priorities — Aboriginal and Torres Strait Islander Histories and Cultures. The collection provides an authentic opportunity for learning and embedding Aboriginal and Torres Strait Islander perspectives because it is written by Aboriginal and Torres Strait Islander people.

We know that children learn better, and enjoy reading more, when they see themselves in the stories, characters and illustrations of the books they read.

To download the app, visit the Google Play Store or Apple Store and search 'Our Yarning'.

You're reading Middle Primary

Learner – Beginner readers

Start your reading journey with short words, big ideas and plenty of pictures.

Level 1 – Rising readers

Raise your reading level with more words, simple sentences and exciting images.

Level 2 – Eager readers

Enjoy your reading time with familiar words, but complex sentences.

Level 3 – Progressing readers

Develop your reading skills with creative stories and some challenging vocabulary.

Level 4 – Fluent readers

Step up your reading skills with playful narratives, new words and fun facts.

Middle Primary – Curious readers

Discover your world through science and stories.

Upper Primary – Adventurous readers

Explore your world through science and stories.

Library For All is an Australian not for profit organisation with a mission to make knowledge accessible to all via an innovative digital library solution. Visit us at libraryforall.org

Bad Big Sister

First published 2024

Published by Library For All Ltd
Email: info@libraryforall.org
URL: libraryforall.org

Our Yarning logo design by Jason Lee, Bidjipidji Art

Original illustrations by Margarita Yeromina

Bad Big Sister
Davies, Kiara
ISBN: 978-1-923339-71-2
SKU04636